I0033779

12 POWERFUL LEADERSHIP AND MANAGEMENT SKILLS

Leadership for Productivity and Project Management

SYED AWAIS RIZVI

Author: Syed Awais Rizvi

Project Manager: Syed Imon Rizvi

Technical Editor: Adeel Mehdi, Alizer Rizvi

Production Manager: Syed Ali Qasim Rizvi

Earlier Publications by Syed Awais Rizvi

#1 Amazon Bestselling Author

"SAP Sales and Distributions Quick Configuration Guide: Advanced SAP Tips and Tricks with Variant Configuration"

Paperback ISBN-10: 1-942554-07-9

Paperback ISBN-13: 978-1-942554-07-3

EBook ISBN-10: 1-942554-02-8

EBook ISBN-13: 978-1-942554-02-8

DEDICATION

I dedicate this book to my mother, father and my supporting wife Sairah along with my family and friends.

ACKNOWLEDGMENTS

I wish to show gratitude dear Ustad Sibtay Jaffer Zaidi as a real example of inspiring leader who still inspire me and many individuals by his legacy of ethics, scholarly works and leadership skills.

Contents

Introduction:

12 Powerful Leadership Skills represent brilliant practical principles for success. This book provide monetary value with short and simple Skills to the reader for fast learning. This book provide tools how to guide with tips and tricks with detailed topic explanation. This book represents extensive focus on complex issues and their answer in the simplest manner. This book resolve into twelve understandable chunk size Skills. Leadership requires systemic approach for business management. Issues can be resolved once or twice but proactive approach to limit the future issues can constitute pose by 12 Effective Leadership & Management Skills.

The skills are guideline for improvement and it is essential is to impose skills its own self for improvement.

12 Effective Leadership & Management Skills shed light on Skills and techniques for learning to sustain edge in self-developing. The guiding principle of 12 Skills based on simple approach. This book can be utilize for leadership or team member who would prove on their skills.

This Book have analyzed the perspective of practical leadership skills for management for any business. Moreover, book also shed some light on information technology software evolution. The 12th guiding principle for the life Improvement skills.

Today's business complexity has increased tremendously with technology and requires heavy empathize of learning of today's complex issue.

Book touch upon subjects that requires greater emphasis on understanding and apply Skills in leadership direction. To realize complex issues require study of what causes these issues to become complex. Understanding of complex issues exhibit us underneath what constitute some of the fundamentals of great leadership skills. For this discovery will assist interpret what cost of the elementary basic issues and how to personify effective leader.

Book provide simple learning guide for Business Analyst. The focused of the book represents the empathize subject with simplification. This book does not offer in-depth and extensive detail about subjects. Book is focus on quick and easy to translate leader management skills.

Part One: Vision

The intellect is a natural disposition which learns from experience.

Imam Ali (a.s) Nahjul Balagah

Part One Summary

Vision represents a goal with anticipation. One can improve their life by envisioning greater good. We can accomplish impossible if one sustain ability to envision, if one imagine the vision then impossible become possible.

Smart Tips to Learn the Vision.

Vision personify the place where we imagine the future.

1. Vision Statement
2. Vision declaration
3. Sample of vision statement
4. Symbolic Vision
5. Lead with Vision

Smart Tips on Brilliant Documentation.

. For documentation consider 6 smart tips and tricks.

1. Documentation
2. Introduction to Documentation
3. Documentation Method
4. Minutes of meeting
5. Minutes of meeting sample
6. Bullet point to "Magic Bullet"

There is no greater wealth than wisdom, no greater poverty than ignorance, no greater heritage than culture, and no greater support than consultation.

Imam Ali (a.s) Nahjul Balagah

1. Vision

Do you have a dream? "I have a dream" phrase represents a symbol of the historical speech by Martin Luther King. Phrase "I have a dream" represents a great example of a vision statement. Statement becomes a vision when expression hold some value, meaning and something better than current state.

Kids starts the imagination with passion of doctor or astronaut, this passion is filled by vision to be. The vision represents desire toward future to imagine to the goal. Vision constitute the imagination of future and regardless of how vision move toward achievement, the team and person involve believe in vision with connection. Vision represented in documented for personal or organizational use. It represents critical for managers to sustain good realization of the Vision.

Vision Statement:

Vision statement puts ideas into words and clarity toward the goal. When vision is not clear, then how it can be utilize? Many ideas are forgotten when we do not write them. Any idea which is not documented might be forgotten. Vision statement over time can be forgotten. At beginning vision statement open a target but it will not explain how it require to be perform. Vision statement is the starting point toward the end goal. How we get to the end goal follow by struggle, determination, innovation, and patience. It is important to define or revise vision statement or explained over and over again to remember it. Vision of any project define the organization or personal goal for improvement. The ROI should personify answer for the vision statement. Vision statement can be closely associated with mission statement. Almost all companies feature mission statement. The mission statement represent the business philosophy. Mission statement true implementation can be observed via reflection on organizations culture and values.

In often case vision statement get lost in regular activities, so for a reminder vision should be in the place where it will be seen frequently. It is like a task list, when we maintain task list but never follow up on it. It require constant systematic approach to follow on the end goal. The solution could be following:

- Daily 2 minutes follow up Vision and reflect what is done and what is required to work on it

- Daily short meeting also can bring up new ideas and issue to work on
- Weekly personal time to reflect on the vision

Vision based on issues:

Issues bring new ideas to improve upon or create new solution. New idea based on issues are good example of lot of innovative and technology visions. Issues can be behind many vision statement for individuals or corporations.

Nothing great was ever achieved without enthusiasm."

Bobby Knight – Henry David Thoreau

There is are many areas where system has limited functionality. The innovation of information technology improve the areas where system has limited functionality.

Vision based on Upgrade:

We as human always want to more. Take an example of new mobile devices, with newer phones faster processors. The need for upgrade represent for improved system with new version of solution. To qualify upgrade please review following self-questionnaire:

- Current product not fast enough.
- Current product not compatible with new software.
- Current Product not functioning properly

Vision Declaration:

Vision statement can be lost easily. I had experienced in forgetting personal vision statement. To remember Vision statement one should setup a way to remind vision statement periodically. I found the best way to remember it by putting it on a wall and reminder on my mobile phone.

Sample of Vision Statement:

Simple vision statement can be written from few lines statement. To review corporation vision statement please review the written vision statement document template. It is sample vision statement used in projects. Start the document with Title. Then the details of who, when and version is updated when is also recorded into the document. Then there is content list according to the document. The content include: introduction, details, stakeholder, product summary etc.

Title of the Vision Document

Prepared by	Date	Version	Notes
Mr. / Ms.	02/16/2016	1.0	

Contents

Introduction 1
Details 2
Environment 3
Stakeholder 4
Product Summary 5

Symbolic Vision:

When vision equal to symbolic vision it can be remembered for long time. When vision own some personal associations it becomes more important. Symbolic vision dedicate some personal tie and something toward better future. To make a vision symbolic add something that represent greater challenge and personal touch for everyone to relate. As a computer or technical savvy people are the massage of vision get lost in tons of documents, keep everyone on track there is a need for symbolic Vision statement. Symbolic statement can be represented by really simple two lines. This symbolic vision should be repeated in all the documents and meetings.

Example of Vision Mission statement: "Create a system with simplicity with improved friendly usability.

Leadership and Vision:

Every person can be effective leader. Effective leader. I can remember few leader who communicated a strong vision.

- Having a strong vision endures great leadership quality.
- Strong leadership envision and communicate their vision

As a leader it is important to remind mission and vision statement to the tram. Vision statement should be incorporated into the name of the project.

- For great impact make vision statement essence into the name of the project.
- Leadership essentially inspire and encourage people toward vision goal.
- Leadership skill help teams to development on vision.

"Imagination is more important than knowledge."

Albert Einstein

2. Documentation, Papers and Records

Introduction to Documentation

From history, until today, document still represents a way of communicating form of massages. The communications haven progressed from cave walls, stone tablets, leather books, paper to electronic file document. Records or books are preserved on paper but computer files consume claim over it. Internet represents new way of Documentation of eBooks and all sorts of records.

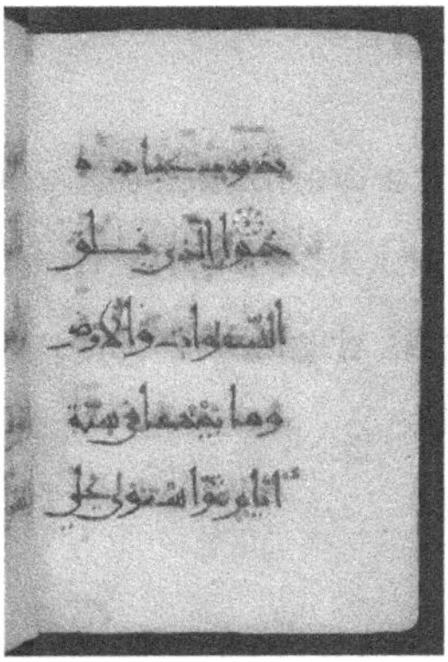

Stone Tablet

Quran Script

Importance of Documentation

We all realize the importance of documentation in our life. Document can connect past, present and future. Without documentation we cannot have proper contracts, agreed discussions, history, books, constitutions, law etc.

- Always note down notes and discussion point
- Document with proper organization of category and catalogs
- Document with reference point and get agreement from all concern parties if involved

To write well, express yourself like common people, but think like a wise man. Or, think as wise men do, but speak as the common people do.
Aristotle

Document with Method:

Always write document with name, subject, date, version etc. Categorization of document becomes easier if the document have followings.

- Title (subject) of the document.
- Name and date on the notes (also can add time to the documents and versions).
- What is required from this document, additional notes etc.
- Make voice notes with smart phone, make file name with date and subject

Tip: The habit of filling document immediately ensures no clutter in future. So filling of document should be done right away.

Lead with Documentation for Business Success

- Successful projects or task have detailed documentations
- Successful project team ensure proper documentation procedures

- Successful project documentation are simple enough for everyone to understand

Assumptions have lots of probability of vagueness that can lead to lot of misunderstanding and miss management. Always document with accountability so everyone stay on same page.

Minutes of Meeting:

I think most meeting are not productive for number of reasons. I have attended many meeting where I was invited for no good reason. Always make sure make meeting are short and have everyone answer if they are required in meeting or not. With market research prove that meeting are not productive. Why we do meet when we are not going to productive. In general regardless of corporate meeting or individual meeting, it is important to write the discussion point, make meetings to the point and invite concern parties. Here are some of the tips for the meeting:

1. Note down all the points discussed in meeting and distribute to all participants for validation.

2. Use document title, participants, dates and versions.

3. Note down follow-up points for next meeting

4. Meeting can be productive with jokes and welcoming environment

Title of the Documents

Date	03/05/2016
Created By	Syed Awais Rizvi
Participants	Mr. Ali, Mr. Sibtay, Mr. Imon
Time	5:00 PM
Agenda	Meeting for book
Document Version	1.0
Notes	Additional Notes
Meeting Location	Online and Room no 786

Agenda: Meeting for book

Meeting Points

- Discussed about book review
- Discussed on eBook editing
- Point 3

Bullet Point to "Magic Pointers"

Built points make complex writing into bite size for readers. Bullet point easy to write and easy to read. Minutes of meeting should be documented in bullet points. It is easy to get bored by reading paragraph or page long descriptions. Bullet points are silver lining messages in bits and pieces. Bullet point should be categorized by subject. Long bullet point kill the purpose of a bullet point, so do not write a paragraph in bullet point.

- Bullet point can make complex subject easy to digestible pieces
- Bullet point are much more easier to read
- **Short and simple** is the key for writing bullet points

Note:

Part Two: Productivity Band Wagon

Summary:

Productivity improved with self-experience and excel with knowledge. Tips for productivity is to keep improving knowledge and skills. Following topics are covered in part two.

Some of the great tips of productivity:

- Meetings with productivity
    - Make Meetings Short
- Solid Agenda
- Productivity with ROI (Return on investment)
- Team Talent Guide
- Simplicity is the best policy

3. Meetings with Productivity

Make Meetings Short:

We all been there when we have long meetings and end up achieving very little. How to make meeting productive? To make meeting productive, make agenda, be precise, element of politeness and humor. The agenda should be simple and short. Short and easy agenda can help participants grasp the purpose to stay on track. Meetings with define agenda with detailed discussion points go long way toward productivity. The discussion points can be communicated to the meeting participants, via call, email or in person discussion.

- Send agenda and question ahead of time
- Send documents to attendees before meeting start
- Send meeting minutes from last meeting
- Call the attendees if possible to discuss the point's needs to be discussed

Firm Agenda

Meeting tend to go off track, when agenda is not communicated well enough. In some cases team member decide to take over the meeting to divert the agenda to fit their needs. The best practice is to communicate the agenda prior to the meeting and also communicate the attendees.

- Emphasis the agenda in the beginning and expectation for the meeting
- Define what is goal of meeting is to everyone
- Define the end goal is expected out of the meeting

Preparation for the Meeting:

Invite concerning people in the meeting and make most of the people optional. By identifying correct and conserving people to the will save lot of wasted time.

- Identify who supposed to be in the meeting before the meeting.
- Share the agenda to the participants
- Call or meet the participants and ask them how can you help them regarding the meting
- Facilitate if participants would like to share their presentation.

Meeting Tips:

- Make people comfortable in meeting and do not start off presentation start with short story or introduction to the meeting.
- Include some jokes in the meeting to make atmosphere welcoming

- Offer participants to ask questions and give extra time for the question or feedback to flow.

"Good teams become great ones when the members trust each other enough to surrender the 'me' for the 'we'"

– Phil Jackson, Basketball

4. ROI Return on Investment:

Introduction to ROI:

ROI stands for return on investment. We calculate ROI on daily life, when we make decision about traffic or decide to take eat healthy. ROI used for decision making to find pros and con and write them on document. ROI documentation benefit to the educated decision making. We calculate the return on investment and pick the best option based on pro and cons. Achieve success by understanding and picking which task is most beneficial toward the end result. Prioritize the task with ROI decision making and pick the best option. When tasks processed with ROI task become more meaningful and less chance of failure.

ROI Template:

This template is provided as sample to understand how ROI document is used for businesses, but it can be used for individuals to calculate the task.

Return on Investment

Prepared by	Date	Version	Description	Notes
Mr. / Ms.	02/16/2016	1.0		

Requirement or need:

Brief Introduction about the ROI topic, for end result.

Pro

Business Benefits Summary:

Brief information about how this will help toward end result.

Estimation of time and efforts:

How many hours are required for this task?	
How many team member are involved in task?	
How frequently this function will be used?	
How this help toward productivity and revenue?	

Pro:

What are the key benefits this process bring to the table?	
How often this function will be used?	

Con:

Point of negative impact	
What new requirements causing effect?	
What are work arounds to complete the task	

5. Team Work

Researches proven that the happy employees have higher productivity. Google is one of the happiest work place and they have highest productivity. Not all the companies have Google approach. Most companies do not invest for happy environment considering the cost but productivity also lost by naïve thinking. Humans look for rewards in nature and they return many times more. Good practice is to praise the whole team instead of individuals, of course there could be high performers but alone they cannot active it is team's effort.

Clear role and responsibilities are essential for team productivity. Imagine if you are part of the team and role and responsibility is unclear then how one can perform without proper role definition. Role and responsibility should be documented and given to the team member. Team need to think together by team building activities, games, challenges, exercise etc. Following are few good tips on team building activities. Team building require a coach who guide them and join them as a team member. Team building exercise can be practiced daily at work even 15 minutes of walk, exercise, games, snacks, quizzes can make a difference for productive team.

All virtue is summed up in dealing justly.

Aristotle

Tips for Team Building Activities:

- **Compete verses cooperation:** encourage team to work together no against each other
- Discouragement always bring unproductivity and encouragement bring more productivity
- Humour bring positive results in team (ethical humour with respect)
- Ethics and politeness should be promoted in team for communication.
- Team building activities like lunch, picnic, walks, sports etc.
- **Team's forum**: for open feedback for any topic and discussion for improvement.
- Clear and solid role and responsibly for each team member

- Be clear to them every team member from the very beginning of the project.

It doesn't make sense to hire smart people and tell them what to do; we hire smart people so they can tell us what to do. Steve Jobs

Team Talent Guide:

It is the common employee who can improve company. So live in close contact with the team and be mindful of their wellbeing. Distribute responsibility with appropriate skillset, interest of individuals. Ask electrician to work on plumbing, can electrician perform productive plumbing? Talent should be based on skillset and experience.

- **Best talent:** Always hire best talent, skilled team member can make a huge difference in organization.

- **For less skilled team member:** Regardless of skill level, best team member could be the one who have "can do it" attitude and persistent.

Ownership Responsibility:

Team member own the responsibility, the sense of ownership without micromanagement creates positive outcomes. When employees feels responsible they take ownership to perform best. Often cases manager try to push the teams instead they should encourage them and see the productive out comes.

Being cheerful and friendly with people is by itself half of wisdom.

Imam Jafar Al-Sadiq (A. S.)   (Behar, vol. 76, p. 60)

Simplicity is the Best Policy:

Technology is increasingly getting complex by day with gadgets, inventions, software and internet of things. Our life are becoming more complex with software's, interfaces, mobile applications and social media etc. Sophisticated software development require greater understanding of complex requirements. The paradigm of complexity is still not clear for huge software developments. Let's take an example of Google, as a search engine software, it is very simple application, user enter the search and get results. If we compare Google with other search engines, their first page is getting complex by day with news, ads and more options. There are many distractions on the page, it take longer time to load and not a clear search results. Google focus on customer first and then other things. Most search engines focuses on ads, news future but not customer. Simple brand product are great in all expects because of usability and friendliness. The software industry has grown into huge number of functions and options but are these functions and option are not used. User want more simple friendly usable software. Most successful software are simple one to use like google or mac computers. If user count number of screens and steps to complete it can turn in to negative feedback and complexity. Complex issues and product development should be simple and friendly.

The most generous person is one who helps the despondent, who does not expect any help from others.

Imam Husain (A.S.)

Note:

Part Three: Business Philosophy

Friendliness philosophy is key to success for business. If we compare all the mobile devices one come to the conclusion of apple phones are dominating mobile market, because apply phones have most friendly features. Also there are phone with similar features but the usability index is not so high, reliability also not high as apple device. So we learn three things from this example.

- Friendliness
- Reliability
- Usability

6. Friendliness

The biggest gap businesses have today is culture of friendliness. Manners and etiquette proven to be key to all business success. If we take example of Japanese culture, it requires Great level off business ethics and friendliness, Japan's economically one of the biggest in the world.

Companies make friendly environment to get the productivity High, take the example of Google, friendly environment make work place more productive. It is win situation for business and employee, company will enjoy high productivity and employee enjoy welcoming environment. To adopt friendly environment is a paradigm shift toward success and productivity.

Reliability and usability.

Product reliability is important to be sustain the market. Toyota is more popular in consumers due to their reliability, so business can make product but cannot make people buy without reliable products.

- Always be reliable for the task and make reliable products
- Make out comes with more usability with reliability

Ethics, Principles and Integrity

Businesses culture with manners, politeness, and joy exceeds the productivity. Employers who empower the employees by provide them good environment benefits from company growth. Google have just done that, google provide employees 20% of time work on anything for innovation and leadership. Giving employee 20% of time toward anything make them leader. Google realize that everyone is leader in their own ways to let them innovate which is never been one before. Innovation not one person job it is team effort to innovate in every step of the way for improvement and success.

Respect should reflect in every aspect of the business. Respect could be associated to everyone so everyone feel they are part of greater cause. Respect should reflect in conversation, email or anywhere communication happens. Ethical certification do not mean the company is ethical, ethics reflect in employee's culture and happiness.

It is important encourage cheerfulness toward others so they feel comfortable, happy environment is created by joy and humor. There are many studies found that happy employee or a person stay productive and stay healthy.

1. Expect nothing from others, instead be best in politeness, courtesy and ethics.
2. Respect others, have polite and respectful interaction with everyone (make them feel good)
3. Cheerful culture promote joyful environment and productivity.

Positive Reinforcement:

It is human nature to expect feel comfort to feel safe and sense of respect and care bring about best of one. People with any high position should always make people under them respected and cared for. Productivity do not grow by force and discouragement. When one feel that company is working for them by rewards, respect and care moral of company goes high and productivity increase.

- Manager always encourage team member to talk freely
- Employees should feel that HR is there for their support

- Open conference should be held to get feedback from representative or individuals without fear of action against them.

Respect and humbleness:

Human nature expect respect and respond to respect with admiration and positive response. Key indicators in business and personal growth, respect is one of the key ingredient. Humbleness is a reflection of adoption of knowledge. When person become humble it represent knowledge in action. Here are few built points on same subject:

1. Practice to use sir names to be respectable
2. Try to have humility with confidence
3. Have a manners and courtesy with kindness

7. Planning and Execute:

To stay productive always schedule daily, weekly and monthly tasks in advance. Preparation bring success of utilization of productive time. Time never stops or return so use of time is indispensable for daily life. Planning is first step toward implementation of the task list. It is easy to plan but more hard to execute the task. Planning to wake up morning is a part of a pan but waking up is execution, if we keep pushing snooze button we are not executing the task on time and that put us on delay on our task.

- Plan weekly activity and daily activity by going over them 5 minutes a day.
- For the best results implement best practice and simple solutions.
- Plan and categorise the tasks in "To-Do" list, and simply follow the task.
- Do not delay any task just follow the ask (no more snooze)

Execute with Methodology:

First step in successful execution to select methodology. Methodology represent successful guide for implementation but each person has their own way method. Implementation should be adopted with the core values to strictly follow the method, with useful track record of implemented. For the success of the execution, methodology methods should be followed.

8. Challenge Approach:

We can safely assume that everyone in project expect successful project. The challenge approach help teams to have fun in their boring workplace! There is phrase that explain the situation:

Break it till you make it!

Facebook organization good example of innovative fun culture. The CEO of Facebook Mike Zuckerberg encourage the challenges, and adopt better solution by anyone. It is a great example of leadership, where good idea prevails. Productive teams open for best solution and suggestions.

If team member are openly challenged to discuss their solution and pick the best solution, it would give edge for huge improvements.

Team challenge Activities:

Encouragement for innovate and challenge better idea. When new idea cannot make in team how this product can sustain the customer needs? There is saying about that "break it till you make it" when product in prototype phase we do test it so see the durability. So the idea should be challenged and tested with team member.

Following activities can be used for team challenge:

- Product marathon (by participating by two or more teams)
- Debate session
- Product proof of concept pros and cons challenge

Best of you, who treat everyone other with respect!

Syed Rizvi

Open Door Policy:

I would also call it open mind approach because it is hard to find leaders who is open to second opinion. Every team member embody creative and innovative in their way. The innovation bring about the change and improvement. Most of companies afraid of innovate with unknown technology. With old traditional business process companies can be carry but cannot compete. To become hesitant toward innovation it will not improve anyone so to improve one must innovate. Google realized the freedom dress something without supervision actually become more productive. Google provide their employees twenty percent of time to work on their own project. In old way to dealing represent to restrict as much possible and monitor every moment of their employee almost close to enslavement. This approach also pass sense of empowerment. If we review an example of apple their team innovate based on new ideas and produce something new.

Note:

Part Four: Risk and Issue Governance

"Nothing will work unless you do"

– John Wooden, Basketball

Risk means danger in future. It exist in all the projects. Risk is always exist before any project starts. How to tackle it depends on project approach. If there is risk and there is nowhere to be communicated it can harm the project. Most managers do not want to hear negative thoughts and face issue because voided the risks communications. The managers who do not want to see risks act like a pigeon.

Interesting fact about pigeon: When cat attack the pigeon to eat, pigeon closes his eyes assuming cat will go away by not seeing her.

It is good practice for project manager to encourage team members to document risk log. It is better to have all the risks documented and communicated to the team member.

And it is not communicated then there might be a chance other team member might miss on fixing it and it can affect the person who did not communicated it.

9. Risk Mitigation

Risk represents possible danger that can be avoided, risks exist in every situations. Risk by definition represent which will be in future. We see risk in daily like; for example traffic on high way, stairs etc. We try to avoid risk and take alternative with less risky alternatives.

- Risk management planning strategy
- Risk monitoring and review process
- Risk should be visible to business and IT for feedback
- Team members should be encouraged to document risks

Risk mitigation can be categorized in following:

Risk Avoidance:

We try to avoid risk in our daily life. Risk always can be avoided when alternatives were adopted and implemented in any given situation.

- Try to find alternatives and perform ROI on given options.
- Known alternatives can bring about known result for risk mitigation.

Risk Management:

If risk management is suppressed then issues will become bigger issue. It is better to be safe than sorry. If risk are identified it should have business case. Risk management should have some standards for risks to be logged. What time period it should be review and worked on.

What it effect and long team effects.

Risk Log Example:

Risk should be maintained in some sort of risk log. There are many tools available for risk and issue tracking. There are some good and bad tools available in market for risk tracking. Risk simple can be tracked in excel sheet too. For the excel ship log here is example for the risk log.

10 Organizational Change Management:

OCM stand for Organizational Change Management. It is human nature when we are exposed something new we are hesitant toward the change out of old habits. When new system get in place it impacts the business process and users because of comfort zone to old system. OCM consultant work on minimizing the business impact. OCM represent more focused from higher management communication plan to the users.

- It is important to understand the vision and have the explanation “why” change is required?

- Start learning about new system or process early and keep the communication from management.
- Start on training early with emphasis with basics

Effective Problem Solving

Problem solving have to deal with issue, what is Issue? Any task which represent a problem for one or more than one person can be called an issue. Issue can be categorized into different levels, it could be that one part of software is not functioning as intended or more than one part having a problem or whole application is not functioning due to number of issues. Issues should be clearly understood. Issue can be solved when we take points from concerning parties or component.

Followings are few good points reading issues management.

- Issues should be documented and communicated to the concerning parties.

- Issue should be tracked and updated periodically.
- Bring All the issues together with team weekly meeting and follow up on them with assigned person

"We can't solve problems by using the same kind of thinking we used when we created them."

Albert Einstein

11. Issue Management

Managing issue strategy should be part of project essential activities. We all have seen when one try to assume there is no issues and close blind eye to the issue. It is good practice to get issued simple as possible and accept the issue. When issues become so complex that team loss the understanding hen it get out of hand. Issues always should be documented even when they are low priority. All the issues should be follow-up and closed appropriately.

There are few different kind s of issues should be considered in project implementation plan.

- Team Issues
- Business Team Issues
- Product development issues
- Change management issues
- Measure and improve the bottom line by measuring issues by accountability

The greatest virtues are those which are most useful to other persons.

Aristotle

12. Powerful Leadership Habits

It is easy to perform a good action, but not easy to acquire a settled habit of performing such actions.
Aristotle

As we can see from Aristotle quote that good actions are easy but making them a habit is very difficult. We can clean out house but if we are asked to make preventing habits that would difficult task to do. If we can learn on out actions to make preventing habit then issues would will be gone. Take an example of pilling up work and then slowly work on it. What if we make a habit to make effort to resolve task as they come along. If tasks are worked upon on the time of appearance then work would not pile up in huge loads. Habit become habit when we practice it periodically.

Productive powerful habits

- Keep happy environment by humour, cheerfulness.
- Focus on energy with time management

- Simplify complex subjects to understand and explain others.
- "Let go of ego" Accept smart idea by others even if you are wrong "Ego never equal to smart"
- Always try to plan early on every task and try to complete them early
- Always be courteous (saying "thank you" and being politeness goes long ways)
- Always be patient and have positive outlook
- Be reasoning with open mind and be humble toward the resolution

If you can't explain it simply, you don't understand it well enough.

Albert Einstein

Certified for
IBM WebSphere.
software

SAP® Certified
Associate

About Author

#1 Amazon Bestselling Author

"SAP Sales and Distributions Quick Configuration Guide: Advanced SAP Tips and Tricks with Variant Configuration"

Syed Awais Rizvi in SAP Project Lead / Architect currently working in automotive industry. He has been a strong Project Lead, and covered numerous SAP project life cycles. He has experience in SAP Project Management, and Implementation. He has worked on upgrade projects, Maintenance projects, template roll-outs and Production Support projects. He has diverse experience in Global implementation of Europe, AIPAC, Middle East and North America from project conception to go-live. He has experience working with Fortune 500 companies. He is SAP SD and SAP Project Management certified.

Connect with him on LinkedIn is at www.linkedin.com/in/syedawaisrizvi you may reach Syed Awais Rizvi via email rrizvir@gmail.com for feedback or query.

Index

www.ingramcontent.com/pod-product-compliance
Lightning Source LLC
Chambersburg PA
CBHW061840220326
41599CB00027B/5353

9781942554073